Michèle Roberts

SILLY LADY NOVELISTS?

dear Lindsey

best wishes —

michèle

D1612269

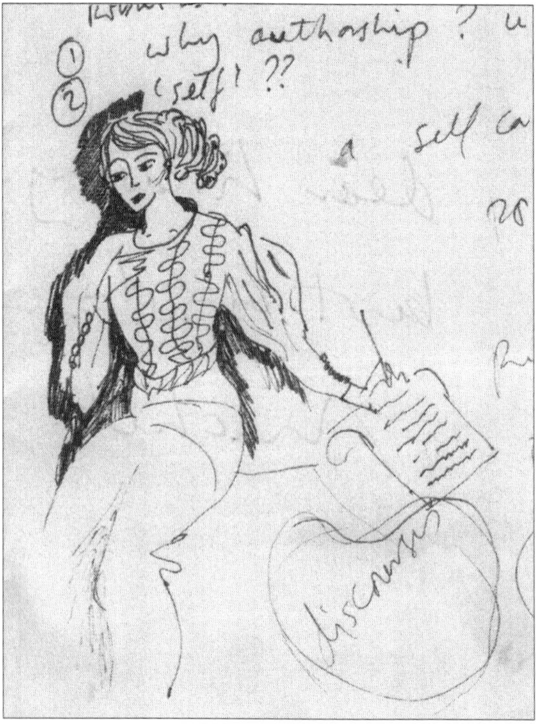

why authorship ?
discourse

Michèle Roberts

SILLY LADY NOVELISTS?

Rack Press Editions

Rack Press Editions is an imprint of Rack Press Poetry

Typeset by CB editions, London
Printed by the Dorset Press
Distributed by Central Books

Published in Wales by Rack Press,
The Rack, Kinnerton, Presteigne, Powys, LD8 2PF
Tel: 01547 560 411
All orders and correspondence:
rackpress@nicholasmurray.co.uk

ISBN 978-0-9931045-9-6

SILLY LADY NOVELISTS?

G eorge Eliot published 'Silly Novels by Lady Novelists' as a review article – what today we'd call a roundup – in the *Westminster Review* in 1856.[1]

Like all her journalism, it was published anonymously, a common practice in those days. Perhaps anonymity allowed her to be super-ferocious. Her witty polemic, 34 pages long, awards the eponymous novels under consider-ation *nul points* one by one.

Recently, by chance, I re-read 'Silly Novels by Lady Novelists', and began to wonder whether it might still be relevant today.

Eliot's blast at 'feminine fatuity' scorches 'a genus with many species, determined by the

---

1. *The Westminster Review*, No 20, October 1856. The essay is reprinted in *Selected Essays, Poems and Other Writings by George Eliot* (Penguin Classics, 1990), edited by A. S. Byatt.

particular quality of silliness that predominates . . . the frothy, the prosy, the pious, or the pedantic. But it is a mixture of all these . . . that produces the largest class of such novels, which we shall distinguish as the mind-and-millinery species.'

Eliot nails the female protagonist of such a tale as inevitably 'the ideal woman in feelings, faculties and flounces.' Way back, in *Pride and Prejudice,* Jane Austen mocked the idea of ladies being universally acclaimed as highly accomplished, and as an example of the sisterhood worth satirising skewered poor Mary Bennet, with her inept piano playing of lengthy concertos at parties and her threadbare philosophising: 'we must pour into the wounded bosoms of each other the balm of sisterly consolation.'

Austen failed to deliver the *coup de grâce*; the type refused to lie down and die. In silly Victorian novels she is re-born, *pace* Eliot, as a heroine with dazzling eyes and wit, 'a superb contralto and a superb intellect; she is perfectly well-dressed and perfectly religious; she dances like a sylph, and reads the Bible in the original tongues.'

This paragon always finds *le mot juste*:

'Rakish men either bite their lips in impotent confusion at her repartees, or are touched to penitence by her reproofs, which, on appropriate occasions, rise to a lofty strain of rhetoric; indeed, there is a gentle propensity in her to make speeches, and to rhapsodise at some length when she retires to her bedroom.' (She generally retires alone, though suitors may lurk outside the door.) Eliot disdains not only this superwoman's sentimental adventures, as she dodges a 'vicious baronet' and tolerates a 'tedious husband' who then conveniently dies, but also her faultless demeanour in emergencies: 'whatever vicissitudes she may undergo, from being dashed out of her carriage to having her head shaved in a fever, she comes out of them all with a complexion more blooming and locks more redundant than ever.'

Eliot distinguishes three main sub-species of silly novels.

First up: 'the oracular', intended 'to expound the writer's religious, philosophical or moral theories . . . there are certain ladies who think that an amazing ignorance, both of science and of life, is the best possible qualification for forming an opinion on the knottiest moral and speculative questions . . . very ordinary events of civilised life are exalted into the most awful crises, and ladies in full skirts and *manches à la chinoise*, conduct themselves not unlike the heroines of sanguinary melodramas'.

Secondly, Eliot picks out 'the white-neckcloth species...a kind of genteel tract on a large scale, intended as a sort of medicinal sweetmeat for Low Church young ladies . . . tender glances are seized from the pulpit stairs instead of the opera-box; tête-à-têtes are seasoned with quotations from Scripture, instead of quotations from the poets; and questions as to the heroine's affections are mingled with anxieties as to the state of her soul.'

Thirdly, Eliot denounces 'the least readable of silly women's novels . . . the modern-antique species' which is full of 'heavy imbecility'. The lady novelists producing this swords-and-sandals guff lack 'imaginative power . . . we find ladies constantly choosing to make their mental mediocrity more conspicuous, by clothing it in a masquerade of ancient names; by putting their feeble sentimentality into the mouths of Roman vestals or Egyptian princesses, and attributing their rhetorical arguments to Jewish high-priests and Greek philosophers.'[2] These silly novels, Eliot warned, only served to confirm 'the popular prejudice against the more solid education of women . . . When men see girls wasting their time in consultations about bonnets and ball dresses, and in giggling or sentimental love-confidences . . . they can hardly help saying, "For Heaven's sake, let girls be better educated: let them have some better objects of thought – some more solid occupations." But after a few hours' conversation with an oracular literary woman, or a few hours' reading of her books, they are likely enough to say, "After all, when a woman gets some knowledge, see what use she makes of it!"'

Such an authoress is irritating morning, noon and night. Eliot ventriloquises such a suffering male: 'She spoils the taste of one's muffin by questions of metaphysics; "puts down" men at a dinner-table with her superior information; and seizes the opportunity of a soirée to catechise

2. Men occasionally wrote such novels too. Flaubert produced *Salammbo*, for example, which seethes with temples and temptresses. When his friends urged him to try something closer to home, the result was *Madame Bovary*. Emma's favourite reading matter is *romans bêtes*.

us on the vital question of the relation between mind and matter. And then, look at her writings! She mistakes vagueness for depth, bombast for eloquence, and affectation for originality; she struts on one page, rolls her eyes on another, grimaces in a third, and is hysterical in a fourth . . . No – the average nature of women is too shallow and feeble a soil to bear much tillage. It is only fit for the very lightest crops."

At the time of writing 'Silly Novels', Eliot herself was one of the most learned women of the day. Girls being routinely denied the schooling offered to their brothers, Eliot had educated herself in science, political thought and literature through solitary study, had taught herself classical and modern languages, had produced translations. If she could do all that, she seems to be asking, why couldn't other women? She ignored the fact that having stayed single, and living in lodgings, she did not have numerous babies to tend, housework to do, meals to provide, a husband to soothe. Perhaps she should have paraphrased Dr Johnson on women preaching sermons and marvelled that women managed to write novels at all. Elizabeth Gaskell, Eliot's contemporary, who was married, with young children, was frank about the difficulties of writing novels while also running a busy household and working in her husband's parish. Since Gaskell believed in the vocation of motherhood existing side-by-side with the vocation of authorship, she did not experience a fundamental conflict between the two. The one enriched the other. She wrote back endearingly to one young would-be female writer, who'd asked her advice, about the importance of being organised over practical tasks such as the laundry: the trick was to have the soaking washing well-soaped. Also, of course, she had servants.

Domestic responsibilities and lack of learning might prevent most lady writers from producing heavyweight tomes on philosophy or mathematics but did not stop truly determined females, even if they skimped on research, from producing fiction. Perhaps unaware of the avalanche of criticism hurtling towards them, oblivious to the likely scorn of learned authorities, ladies continued to produce their silly books.

But why did so many ladies want to write novels in the first place? Eliot dismisses the notion that 'destitute women turned novelists, as they turned governesses, because they had no other "ladylike" means of getting their bread. On this supposition, vacillating syntax and improbable incident had a certain pathos for us . . . Empty writing was excused by an empty stomach, and twaddle was consecrated by tears.' Not the case, she decides. These 'fair writers' must have cushy lives. They 'have obviously never talked to a tradesman except from a carriage window . . . they have no feeling of interest in any man who is not at least a great landed proprietor, if not a prime minister. It is clear that they write in elegant boudoirs, with violet-coloured ink and a ruby pen; that they must be entirely indifferent to publishers' accounts, and inexperienced in every form of poverty except poverty of brains.'

Surely you might be from the shabbiest of backgrounds yet still choose to write about dukes? Eliot herself had yet to get cracking on her groundbreaking realist novels of yeoman life. Her remarks were in any case inaccurate. In *A Literature of Their Own*[3] Elaine Showalter

3. Elaine Showalter, *A Literature of Their Own: British Women Novelists from Brontë to Lessing* (Yale, 1977).

pointed out that in the nineteenth century whereas 'most male writers had other professions and sources of income . . . middle-class women had very few alternative occupations to writing.' Many, brisk and practical, also found openings 'in the business end of publishing; many also worked as publishers' readers and copy-editors.' They took all these jobs seriously: 'women writers were likely to be dependent on their earnings and contributing to the support of their families, and not, as has been conjectured, indulging themselves at the expense of fathers and husbands.'[4]

Eliot did respect the works of some of her female contemporaries. She admired George Sand's pioneering novels, also those by Harriet Martineau, Currer Bell (Charlotte Bronte) and Elizabeth Gaskell. Perhaps 'Silly Novels by Lady Novelists' simply shows Eliot, like many another ambitious beginner writer of fiction, setting out her stall and slapping away the competition: she's not going to write like *those* flim-flam, flimsy-whimsy performers. Deriding the results of the paltry education doled out to her

4. Showalter, *op.cit.*, pp. 46–7.

female contemporaries, she prides herself on her exceptional status. Although she wanted women generally to be better educated, she wasn't a feminist who criticised the prevailing system of male privilege and entitlement. Rather, she believed in men and women companionably evolving together. She didn't openly protest at the double standard of her day, which meant that learned women could be mocked as monstrous, ugly blue-stockings (she herself was routinely labelled hideous and 'masculine') while uneducated ones were written off as deliciously fluffy airheads.

She did, though, satirise gender prescriptions. For example, Mr Brooke, in *Middlemarch*, feels anxious about his niece Dorothea's ardent wish for learning, because it's not necessary for nice girls expected to make good marriages. Lacking learning, Dorothea over-reveres men who have it, and so marries the withered pedant Casaubon. Simultaneously, Lydgate, fascinated by pretty, blue-eyed Rosamond Vincy's adorable naïveté, so flattering to his ego, finds out too late that this conceals manipulativeness, coldness and deceit. Rosamond, a 'young sylph' fresh out of finishing-school, has learned only the art of hooking a man and thinks her brother's quotations of images from Homer are 'slang'.

E liot didn't mock silliness in lady writers only when she wrote journalism. She helpfully provided a portrait of a silliness-producing lady scribe in *Daniel Deronda* (1876), amongst a gallery of images of the woman artist: actress, musician, singer- and writer. One problem structuring women's dilemmas in this novel concerns public and private spheres, the former seen as belonging to men and the latter as belonging to women- for the middle classes at least. On the one hand Eliot, via her hero Deronda, seems to be dismayed by the ruthless commitment of the professional actress/singer Alcharisi, Deronda's mother, the star who has rejected her son as a child in order to display her gifts out in the world and hog the limelight. On the other hand Eliot derides the incompetence of the self-deluding amateur, the nouveau-riche Mrs Arrowpoint, who strives to combine scribbling with being a successful county hostess.

Comedy erupts when Eliot's heroine Gwendolen Harleth attends a soiree given by the Arrowpoints at Quetcham, their big country house. The 'lady of Quetcham' has 'a squat figure, a harsh parrot-like voice, and a systematically high head-dress; and since these points made her externally rather ridiculous, it appeared to many only natural that she should have what are called literary tendencies.'

Poor Mrs Arrowpoint produces only 'feeble literature'. Gwendolen assumes 'that because Mrs Arrowpoint was ridiculous she was also likely to be wanting in penetration' and proceeds to tease her: 'I wish I could write books to amuse myself, as you can! How delightful it must be to write books after one's own taste instead of reading other people's! Home-made books must be so nice!'

Her hostess chooses to believe in her guest's 'girlish simplicity' rather than 'satire' when Gwendolen adds: 'I would give anything to write a book!' Mrs Arrowpoint replies: 'you have but to begin as I did. Pen, ink and paper are at everybody's command.' She has so far produced many 'sheets in manuscript' and confides: 'These are things I daresay I shall publish eventually: several friends have urged me to do so, and one doesn't like to be obstinate. My Tasso, for example – I could have made it twice the size.' Is Mrs Arrowpoint writing a novel? It seems so, to some extent: 'I have constructed the early part of his life as a sort of romance.' Eliot's mockery peaks in one marvellous brisk sentence: '"I dote on Tasso," said Gwendolen.'

The question wasn't simply one of talent. Stern man-made rules about suitable feminine subjects and styles constricted many nineteenth-century lady writers keen to avoid thunderous denunciation from male pundits in pulpit and periodical. In 'Silly Novels' George Eliot mocks the resulting weak fiction but ignores the social and moral imperatives shaping it.[5] These derived from Christianity.

Christianity is a male religion founded on men's fear of death. Since sex with women led to

5. For more examples of what Eliot ignored, see Patricia Duncker's witty novel *Sophie and the Sibyl: A Victorian Romance* (2015).

the birth of babies, and since having been born meant that you would eventually die, according to patriarchal logic women were to blame for the fact of death, their sexuality accordingly seen as dangerous and hateful. Hence the theology of the magical Virgin Birth of the Son of God, with its concomitant denial of maternal-sexual power. God could not be allowed by the fretting patriarchs to be born of an ordinary woman. Mary, the exception, was a virgin; a mere container not actively involved in conception. The resurrection showed Christ triumphing over death and also, therefore, over the female body.

If men absolutely had to have sex, they could marry. Women were to blame for men's lust but also satisfied it, as wives or lovers/prostitutes, the former tolerated and the latter condemned. Control of female sexuality was key to Christianity down the centuries. Holiness was split from sexiness. Virginity got you fast-tracked to heaven after death.

Just as Catholic theology strictly divided Virgins from Whores, so Victorian critics, openly Protestant or nominally agnostic, distinguished Good women (who pretended they had never

16

heard of sex) from Bad ones (who mentioned it). Unmarried Good women writing novels could be mocked for their ignorance of Real Life. Married Good women writing novels were supposed to gloss over their knowledge of the facts of life. Any woman who wrote explicitly about passion couldn't be Good but was obviously Bad. For example, Charlotte Bronte, once she'd been outed as a female writer after having hidden behind the masculine mask Currer Bell to publish *Jane Eyre,* was vilified as grossly unfeminine, coarse and corrupt. Later, Elizabeth Gaskell, writing her friend's biography, felt the need to stress Bronte's admirable qualities as dutiful daughter and churchgoer and to omit the fact that Charlotte had passionately loved a married man. Gaskell herself ran into big trouble when, in *Ruth* (1853), she dared to write sympathetically about an unmarried mother.

I f the hordes of genteel lady novelists obeyed explicitly spelled-out notions of feminine propriety derived from Christian teaching, accordingly created goody-goody heroines, and so could be patted on the head as Good and see their books simultaneously dismissed as Silly, more brazen fantasists explored female rage and desire through the medium of sensationalist fiction featuring devil-women cheerfully committing adultery, arson and murder. Such novels really got the critics spluttering over the 'foulest...confessions of the darkest profligacy that an utter reprobate could make'[6]

In North America, Louisa M. Alcott produced both sorts of writing at once. Obeying the Virgin/Whore dichotomy, she kept her Good and Bad writing selves severely separate. She is best known for her saccharine, preachy tale *Little Women* (1868), its cosy mother-plus-daughters ménage prefiguring the equally sentimentalised Meyrick household in Eliot's *Daniel Deronda*. She published *Little Women* under her own name, whereas her various tales of sashaying, murderous, drug-addicted heroines were published using a nom de plume.

Elaine Showalter, discussing the British sensationalists,[7] argues that where Wilkie Collins,

6. Francis Paget, quoted by Elaine Showalter, *op.cit.*, p. 160.
7. Showalter, *op. cit.*, p. 153 *et seq.*

often presumed to have invented the genre, relies on 'relatively conventional . . . social and sexual attitudes', the female sensationalists 'revised and challenged' those conventions, and indeed exploited them thrillingly. Rejecting the pattern of 'self-sacrificing masochism in George Eliot', a novelist such as Mary Braddon allowed her heroines to 'take over the properties of the Byronic hero.'

Braddon's *chef d'oeuvre* is *Lady Audley's Secret* (1862). The novel opens with the description of a country estate and a house conveniently filled with Gothic 'secret chambers' and a hiding-place beneath the floorboards in a certain room, also a disused well in the grounds, handy for throwing corpses down. We learn that Sir Michael Audley, a widower, has recently re-married, choosing an ex-governess who is always 'lighthearted, happy and contented.' She skips about, visiting the poor, 'apparently as pleased with the admiration of a toothless crone as if she had been listening to the compliments of a marquis . . . For you see Miss Lucy Graham was blessed with that magic power of fascination by which a woman can charm with a word or intoxicate with a smile.'

Sweetie-pie Lucy seems to be a blessed damozel dropped from heaven: she is blessed with 'the most wonderful curls in the world – soft and feathery, always floating away from her face, and making a pale halo round her head when the sunlight shone through them.' Alas: tears ensue after bedtime. Gradually, Lucy is stripped of the layers of her disguises and finally fully revealed in all her wickedness.

In *Lady Audley's Secret* the madwoman is no longer confined to the attic but slinks downstairs into the drawing-room. As Showalter puts it: 'Braddon makes her would-be murderess the fragile blond angel of domestic realism . . . The dangerous woman is not the rebel or the bluestocking but the "pretty little girl" whose indoctrination in the female role has taught her secrecy and deceitfulness, almost as secondary sex characteristics. She is particularly dangerous because she looks so innocent.'

Ignoring the outrage of Christian critics, Victorian readers were entranced. They 'responded by making the novel one of the greatest successes in publishing history: there were eight editions the first year alone, and it was never out of print during Braddon's lifetime.' Braddon's novel, says Showalter, has been 'much under-rated'. Until pioneering scholars like Showalter rescued it, *Lady Audley's Secret* was either ignored by twentieth-century critics with proper notions of Good Writing, or simply flicked into the Silly/feminine category. That came to pretty much the same thing.

T he second wave of feminism, beginning in the late 1960s, saw female scholars reassessing the male-written, male-dominated literary canon and arguing that it should include more women writers. This wasn't just a numbers game. The omission of female writers meant a falsification and simplification of a complex literary history. One result of the turbulent theory wars of the 1980s (a text is just a text, a smile is just a smile . . .) was that as certain non-canonical texts began to be studied, so more kinds of writing by women got reassessed, including their sensationalist fiction. This had been seen as lowbrow not least because it was often reminiscent of popular melodrama, very pleasing to readers stuck at home and yearning for adventures; if you couldn't get out much, theatre could come to you. Mary Braddon had a background in theatre, which *Lady Audley's Secret* demonstrates, with its tortuous plot, red herrings, and delight in disguises. As a result of how Braddon wrote, according to some critics she is a Bad writer. As a result of what she wrote about, some of her contemporaries saw her as a Bad woman.

S ince ladies often wrote silly novels, a log- ic began to prevail which suggested that, their books becoming elided with their persons, they then became silly lady novelists, silly just because they wrote at all. Spinsters were silly, because they did not have men to rein them in. Spinsters writing novels were very silly indeed, especially if they aped the men they lacked. Miss Lavish, in E. M. Forster's *A Room With a View* (1908), a New Woman who wears 'a blue military cloak', strides alone about the 'dear dirty' backstreets of Florence gathering material for her new book. She despises her fellow tourists who sightsee in organised groups, and patronises the locals: 'Look at that adorable wine-cart! How the driver stares at us, dear simple soul!' Taking young Lucy Honeychurch sightseeing, chatty Miss Lavish gets lost in her wandering sentences, and gets simultaneously lost, an accidental *flâneuse*, en route to Santa Croce: 'you are *not*, *not*, *not* to look at your Baedeker. Give it to me; I shan't let you carry it. We will simply drift.'

Miss Lavish, proclaiming herself resolutely unconventional, relishes 'plain speaking, and meeting different grades of thought.' Back at the *pensione* she is discovered to be a smoker of cigarettes. 'A good fellow, Lavish, but I wish she'd start a pipe' says droll Mr Beebe. He tells Lucy the tale of how Miss Lavish, having taken two fellow guests, the Emersons, father and son, to be 'commercial travellers', boldly pursued them after dinner one night into the smoking-room to show them how charmingly unprejudiced she was: 'At the end of five minutes she returned unobtrusively with a green baize board and began playing Patience.' Lucy asks what happened. Mr Beebe replies: 'No one knows. No one will ever know. Miss Lavish will never dare to tell'.

Cowardly Miss Lavish does dare to tell a

secret belonging to Lucy, conveyed by gossipy Miss Bartlett, Lucy's chaperone on the Italian trip. Lucy has begged the older woman not to betray her and Miss Bartlett flouts her promise not to do so. The secret has to do with sex, and therefore Miss Lavish's putting it, in a disgracefully unfeminine way, into the public sphere, shames Lucy, whose virginal reputation stands to be ruined.

Earlier, Miss Bartlett expounds the rules George Eliot's Dorothea Brooke came up against. Lucy wonders 'why were most big things unladylike?' Miss Bartlett explains: 'It was not that ladies were inferior to men; it was that they were different. Their mission was to inspire others to achievement rather than to achieve themselves. Indirectly, by means of tact and a spotless name, a lady could achieve much. But if she rushed into the fray herself she would be first censured, then despised, and finally ignored. Poems had been written to illustrate this point.'

Masculine Miss Lavish, breaking these rules of femininity, is also, we are not surprised to hear, a bad writer. Although she daringly introduces sex into her new novel she lacks imagination as she lacks experience, and so her 'draggled prose' draws on silly Miss Bartlett's gossip about Lucy having been kissed by George Emerson: 'Leonora sat pensive and alone. Before her lay the rich champaign of Tuscany, dotted over with many a smiling village . . . Afar off the towers of Florence, while the bank on which she sat was carpeted with violets. All unobserved, Antonio stole up behind her- there came from his lips no wordy protestation such as formal lovers use. No eloquence was his, nor did he suffer from the lack of it. He simply enfolded her in his manly arms.' This soppy passage nonetheless acts as a turn-on: hearing it read aloud at a tennis party by supercilious snobbish Cecil, Lucy's foolishly-chosen fiancé, and recognising its source, George gets fired up, follows Lucy up the garden path and kisses her again. She flees him and then, trying to deny that she fancies him, threatens to leave home and 'share a flat for a little with some other girl', in her mother's words to 'mess with typewriters and latchkeys . . . And agitate and scream, and be carried off kicking by the police.' Becoming a Suffragette is as bad as being Miss Lavish. But everything ends suitably: Lucy and George marry and silly novelist Miss Lavish fades away.

After the Great War, the New Women did not fade but bloomed. Modernists such as Katherine Mansfield, Virginia Woolf and Dorothy Richardson began breaking literary rules and inventing new literary forms. To do so, some of them also broke rules of femininity and invented new female selves. Some stayed single, testing new freedoms. Flouting Christian morality, some had love affairs with other women or, like Rose Macaulay, secret love affairs with married men.[8] Many nipped off to Paris to hobnob with other Bohemians, visit lesbian salons such as that run by the American poet Nathalie Barney and frequented by rising stars such as Colette, and generally enjoy a non-stuffy literary culture.

Not everyone, of course, could or did act out rebellion in this way. Working-class women who wanted to write had enormous odds stacked against them.[9] They had a long struggle before their voices became widely heard.

8. Sarah LeFanu argues in her biography of Rose Macaulay (2003) that this arrangement left Rose free of domestic tasks and childcare and able to concentrate on her writing.

9. See Kenneth Rose, *The Intellectual Life of the British Working Classes* (2001).

Outside boho-chic coteries such as the Bloomsbury group, a married middle-class woman who wrote novels might need to be humorously self-deprecating about her literary work in order to conceal her unfeminine commitment to it. She might need to hide her ambition, the ruthlessness required for writing, behind a ruched cloak of velvety modesty. Such a one is the narrator of E. M. Delafield's *Diary of a Provincial Lady* (1930). The silly lady novelist now provides her own self-portrait.

Writing the introduction to the reissued Penguin version of Delafield's novel, Rachel Johnson (herself a novelist from a posh background) considers that the eponymous diarist is 'the first woman in fiction, and perhaps the first woman ever, to "have it all"', as modern women supposedly do (a cliché meaning that women should not complain). She certainly has it all to contend with: a grumpy, taciturn husband who ignores her; fussy, inquisitive neighbours such as the Vicar's (nameless) wife; time-consuming, boring social duties; worry about her darling young children at boarding-school; not enough suitable hats for garden parties; little solitude for writing; bothersome servants.[10] Through her clever choice of form, Delafield makes cosy comedy out of the marriage trap, the repressions forced upon her long-suffering heroine. The eponymous diary holds all that she is forbidden and forbids herself to say; very consoling for Delafield's similarly placed female readers. In our time characterised by nostalgia for the 1950s, cupcakes and frilly aprons, alongside bourgeois anxiety about dysfunctional families and unmarried mothers and distaste for whingeing women, Delafield's novel has glided back into fashion. Behind the wry, self-denigrating quips and jokes we may detect half-stifled screams of rage, but the narrative style – *toujours la politesse* – lets us pretend we haven't heard them.

I n *The Second Sex* (1949) Simone de Beauvoir argued that men saw themselves as human and women as sexed and that they inscribed

10. Alison Light brilliantly reveals the handmaidens' point of view in *Mrs Woolf and the Servants: The Hidden Heart of Domestic Service* (2007).

women as the Other.

Biologically speaking, *she* had once contained *him*, but philosophically, by a patriarchal sleight of hand, it was the other way round. Femaleness could not represent humanity. *She* could not include *he*.[11]

For a founding example of maleness swallowing femaleness we must take another look at Christianity, still going strong when De Beauvoir was writing.

The Christian myth featured a male Saviour who took over female functions and performed them better than mere women ever could. Christ, supposedly sexless in his lifetime, was subsequently credited with a magically pregnant body, his flesh and blood renewed during Mass, in the miracle of Transubstantiation, to nourish the faithful, who were eventually re-born into eternal life. His agony on the cross aped that of childbirth. His capacity to give birth was pure and uncontaminating, unlike that of women: in the ceremony of churching, women just out of childbed were forgiven by male priests for the

11. Of course, *man* could be sexed when necessary, as in traditional love poetry.

sin of sex that had led to pregnancy, and were ritually cleansed of their dirtiness.

Spirit, the anxious patriarchs preached, was superior to body and supposedly ruled it. Man got lined up with spirit and woman with body. Accordingly, men were supposed to rule over women.

De Beauvoir argued that women, as the Other, could only act out being feminine or un-feminine. Femininity, apparently artless and innate, was actually learned and rehearsed, less a manifestation of your deepest, realest being than a psychic costume you donned in order to pass muster with the master. Surrealist male artists might rave about women's eternal mystery, her naturalness and closeness to the unconscious, but a writer like Anais Nin knew very well how to arrange her own veil, how to pose for the male gaze, smuggling in her sharply pointed fantasies under fragrant heaps of flowery adjectives. You might well have some fun with femininity, and indeed derive great pleasure from it, frocks and high heels and charm being lovely when you were in the mood for them, but you couldn't not be that specifically gendered creature. (De Beauvoir herself opted for lipstick, chic little skirts and turbans and deplored the unfeminine scruffiness of many of her young female admirers.) Colette, De Beauvoir's contemporary, wittily explored femininity in her earliest short stories, depicting bourgeois women scurrying between those contemporary priests: couturier, masseur, coiffeur, chiropodist, lingerie-maker, dietician, etc. Colette's laughter! It's the laughter of the Sphinx.

Certain 1970s feminists (there were different kinds – they came in different shapes, like Liquorice Allsorts) developed de Beauvoir's ideas and argued that gender was not the same as sex, femininity being simply a set of imposed characteristics, shifting from time to time according to necessity; for example it could include making armaments in factories in wartime. If having a womb didn't automatically make you a goddess (which some Liquorice Allsorts yearned for) it didn't mean you were naturally prone to hysteria and/or a love of corsets either.

Over in France, philosopher Julia Kristeva and others developed the notion of *écriture féminine,* which disobeyed what Kristeva named the Law of the Father. This Law was the either/or binary code imposed on children learning to speak and write correctly, which was embodied in conventional grammatical rules of subject-verb-object. *Écriture féminine* broke these rules in order to invoke the poetic babble of the child to the mother (a kind of language subsequently repressed by authority figures), therefore our unconscious, playful, illogical, emotional life. Men too could write *écriture féminine*. Kristeva cited James Joyce. I'd add in James Kelman.

In the early 1970s, feminist publishers such as Virago, the Women's Press, Sheba, Onlywomen, Honno, etc, began publishing new fiction by women that challenged the old categories of suitable/unsuitable subjects and styles. This built on fiction written in the previous generation by writers such as Nell Dunn, Margaret Drabble, Maureen Duffy, Beryl Bainbridge *et al.*

Women's writing could now mean *subversive writing*, provocative rather than preacherly, realist as well as poetic, fiction of the sort produced by Angela Carter, Emma Tennant, Sara Maitland, Christine Brooke-Rose, Marina Warner, Alison Fell and other iconoclasts. Some of them explored Otherness, but on their own terms. Some of them put new wine in new bottles. The feminist presses also published fiction by female writers from the rest of Europe, the Caribbean, Africa, Asia, North and South America. The literary landscape was enlarged, freshly mapped and newly imagined. No wonder feminist science fiction flourished, asking seriously playful *what-if* questions.[12] Hostile critics could of course dismiss *women's writing* and caricature its authors as unfeminine humourless harridans and duly did so.

Non-feminist women writers of popular fiction aimed at a predominantly female market continued being categorised in the feminine/silly tradition, their works disparaged by journalists as Aga-sagas, bonkbusters, bodice-rippers, sex'n'shopping, etcetera. (Certain writers in this tradition, such as Jackie Collins, have become rediscovered and championed as cult heroines.)

Non-feminist women writers ambitious to succeed in the mainstream literary world alongside men and avoid being pushed into the pigeonhole of Otherness could flee the derogatory feminine

12. See Sarah LeFanu, *In The Chinks of the World Machine: Feminism and Science Fiction* (1988), which discusses the fiction produced by, among others, Ursula Le Guin, Suzy McKee Charnas, Joanna Russ and James Tiptree Jr.

label by denying their femaleness altogether, as the Brontes and later Eliot herself had done.[13] They could hide behind ambiguous initials (a strategy still employed by some female writers today). Just like the female saints of Christian tradition they could try to transcend their sexed bodies, their gendered inferior status. In Christ there was supposedly no male or female, was there? So these writers could insist that artists were androgynous or genderless spokespersons (ahem! spokes*men*) for humanity. That was what male writers said of themselves, after all. Did the strategy succeed?

Most male writers did not feel the need anxiously to conceal their sex in the same way, since man represented both humanity and male sexed beings.[14] Men who chose to use initials still seemed male.

Critics complained that the silly feminists simply didn't understand how the word *man*

13. Eliot had an especial reason for concealment: she was living with a married man and therefore likely to be read and judged as morally disgusting.

14. They could hide it when larkin' about: the Hull librarian, writing Trinianesque porno about schoolgirls, invented a female pseudonym to make the porn more fun.

worked. It included women! *Man* was a mam-
mal who suckled his young! Feminists retorted
that, given men's social and financial power,
the two meanings of man got elided. As a result, men could see themselves as objective and
authoritative rather than as male and partial.

S uch sticky tangles around gender could,
nonetheless, provide fabulous inspiration
and material for fiction and fantasy. Even within an ostensibly silly/feminine genre such as the
romance, subversion could be at work.

As an adolescent struggling within the femi-
nine/unfeminine trap, often feeling like a female
impersonator (many of my contemporaries, I
later discovered, felt similarly), I found consolation in Georgette Heyer's historical romances
featuring heroines dressing up as boys in order
to escape convention and gain freedom. In my
favourite of Heyer's romps, *The Masqueraders*
(1928), set in eighteenth-century London, both
sexes cross-dress. We encounter a brother and
sister, Mr and Miss Merriott, Peter and Kate,
members of the gentry, he appropriately fine

in riding boots and embroidered gauntlets and she exquisitely pretty in 'a taffety gown of blue spread over a wide hoop . . . her fair ringlets in *demi-toilette*, free from powder, with a blue ribbon threaded through, and a couple of curls allowed to fall over her shoulder.'[15]

Peter is in fact Prudence, and Kate is in fact Robin. The reason for their disguise is that they are escaped Jacobins with a price on their heads. Attentive to its female readership, the novel concentrates its sexual comedy on Prudence, striding out in velvet breeches and powdered wig to enter gaming saloons, listen to men's sexy talk, swig buckets of claret, draw her sword and fight off muggers, challenge villains to duels, escape the Bow Street Runners when accused of murder, and, perhaps as a respite from all this, flirt with other women.

The story, indeed, flirts with the reader. It upends convention while finally reasserting it. Prudence's masquerade is revealed to us once

15. *The Masqueraders* was published in the same year as Virginia Woolf's experimental novel of sexual shapeshifting, *Orlando*. I imagine Heyer and Woolf discussing narrative technique over tea. Alas, their diaries do not mention that momentous meeting.

she has met the tall, burly, sternly handsome Sir Anthony and immediately fallen for him, just as in the same episode Robin meets the deliciously girly Laetitia and falls for her, but we don't know, until he tells Prudence over a tête-à-tête dinner, quite when Sir Anthony has pierced her disguise. The novel's play with concealment and unmasking dramatises a young woman's wish not to be objectified but truly seen, truly known. Its romantic and sexy appeal resides in its stirring hints of bisexuality. Re-reading it, I notice how Heyer describes Prudence as a 'slim . . . stripling' when she's in drag, but 'big' and 'stately' when she's back in a frock.

S o what about ladies' silly novels *de nos jours*? Do any novels by women get labelled in that way today? Surely we've gone beyond those silly categories?

Who needs Kristeva now? Surely in this glorious post-feminist world women are free to say, do and be whatever they want, and so female writers can write novels ditto and never be judged as women but only as human beings, only as writers, and so any discussion about gender and writing is unnecessary and indeed silly and I should just shut up.

I think that in the changed literary world we now inhabit, gender matters as much as it ever did. Why? Because of money. With the triumph of the international free market, novels have become commodities whose worth is measured in the money they make; their literary worth is secondary, or rather, derives/begins to derive from sales figures.[16] All writers are now under pressure to produce bestsellers appealing to a mass market. Many are called but few are chosen. Sophisticated, costly publicity and marketing campaigns help. Bookshop chains charging publishers for display space point out that they are running businesses, not charities. The novelists who repeatedly manage to reach the top of the list become brands.

16. I am indebted to Amit Chaudhuri for this perception about financial and literary value, which he expressed elegantly and at length in a lecture at UEA in the mid 2000s.

Some of us may still think we can recognise good writing when we see it, but we're increasingly encouraged to suppose that's merely a matter of personal taste. You just have to *like* something. Click! Sometimes a circular logic prevails: because X sells well, he or she must be a good writer; therefore he or she sells well.

To call a novel *literary* is to insult it: it is not *commercial*. The new binary code! Some commercially successful writers feel cross at being thought of as unliterary and some literary ones feel cross at their supposed lack of popular appeal. Some literary writers straddle the divide and sell well. (George Eliot thought of writing as a vocation, which carried moral responsibility, but she cared a lot about being decently paid, too. She didn't, as Patricia Duncker once pointed out to me, have to sell in lorryloads in order to be seen as successful in both literary and commercial terms.)

Since novels are apparently just like tinned tomatoes, individual makes must be distinguished amongst the competition and the notion of difference invoked, to help the discriminating shopper exercise free choice and decide what to consume.

Femininity returns, as a selling point.

As any fule kno, women buy, borrow and read more books than men do. Women are generous, tolerant readers, often happily hopping back and forth between literary and popular fiction, happily reading all sorts of novels along the literary-to-thriller spectrum by women and also by men (who don't always return the compliment and read women's books). However, women readers are supposed by many agents and marketing persons to long only for certain sorts of commercial fiction written in a brisk international vernacular aping that employed in celebrity memoirs. George Eliot might call these novels silly; that's an outmoded category these days. What matters is sales figures.

Plus ça change? The old simplistic notions of Good and Bad, heroines and anti-heroines, remain. A lack of ambiguity makes for easier reading and more sales. For example, feminism-lite can inform whimsical, unthreatening, often self-mocking tales (post-post-*Bridget Jones* and its super-clever rendering of feminine angst) of feisty but fond females tackling domestic and sexual upsets with the help of daffy girlfriends, well-meaning stepfamilies, boys next door, etcetera. These read, on one level, as etiquette manuals on how to steer towards or through modern marriage, and remind us how one root of the eighteenth-century English novel was magazines' agony columns.

Another, opposite type of commercially attractive tale follows the tradition of the sensationalist novels of Eliot's day and features women behaving Badly. However, the protagonists' implicit resentment is directed less against manmade rules of conduct than against womanly notions of sisterhood. Women are presented as backstabbing, bitchy competitors for male attention, sex and money. A backlash against feminism, perhaps, feminism being written off as the boring new version of Goodness, to be resisted. Now, having it all can mean enjoying stealing it. One debut novelist (her book apparently a bestseller pre-publication, the film rights already sold) recently claimed to have written 'Iago with tits.' Whoopee!

Despite the fact that new, non-binary identities for human beings are being claimed as fast as you can say no-platforming, literary agents hungry for fresh talent continue to invent niche categories of readership according to Otherness.

Women's psychological realism. Women's domestic thrillers. Women's noir. Chicklit. Griplit. Women's erotica. Female Young Adult. Female Fantasy. Etcetera.

Writers may fume at their original, carefully written books aimed at *tout le monde* being shoved into gendered pigeonholes simply for commercial reasons but the agents don't care. Some writers ignore the pigeonholing. Some actively, cynically court it, researching the market and tailoring their work to fit.

One recent form of breakout from the absurd labelling is evidenced by writers such as Jackie Kay, Ali Smith, Sarah Waters and Jeanette Winterson. They don't necessarily resemble each other as writers, and I'm sure would not want to be seen as members of a group, but nonetheless their lesbian identities have become part of their literary appeal. They enact a third term, queer and shapeshifting. Like the female modernists of the 1920s they live differently and write differently and readers lap up their work.

O ne way to avoid the feminine trap might be not to put the word Girl in your title. *Girl With a Pearl Earring* by Tracy Chevalier. OK. Her bestseller began it. But she has been imitated too often.

Young *woman* presumably just doesn't have that marketeers' snap crackle and pop. Best to avoid *woman* whenever possible. *Woman* sounds too grown up! Porno-merchants offer girls as desirable merchandise, after all.

P orn used to be for chaps and romance for the ladies. The one complemented the other. Just like masculine and feminine yeah! In these postmodernist days, genres blur and overlap, despite the best policing efforts of the marketing persons. For example, men write romances buried inside thrillers (the emotionally scarred detective who doesn't dare to trust women). Similarly, aspects of porn have become explicit in romance. Porn and romance share a source; both eroticise sexual inequality, which becomes *the* source of pleasure.

Take the porno-romance *Fifty Shades of Beige*.

Take it rapidly: it is very badly written and frightfully repetitive and boring but you'll get the gist. If you let a man hurt you enough he will reward you with a fitted kitchen.

Why did *Beige* sell so many millions of copies? Do millions of women long to be hurt? Another proof of Eliot's 'feminine fatuity'?

The sales figures suggest that Christianity remains alive and kicking. The Church channelled young women's longings for adventure into acceptable wishes for holiness. For example, a medieval woman who abandoned her husband and children and hit the road had to protest that she was just going on pilgrimage.[17] The trials in *Beige* resemble those in medieval Lives of Saints: virgins thrown naked into brothels and raped; wives tortured by their despotic husbands. God rewards these longsuffering martyrs with a place in heaven. These stories circulated also as folk tales such as Patient Griselda,[18] and so now the popular *Beige*.

17. See Margery Kempe's account of her travels in her *Booke*.
18. See Marina Warner, *From the Beast to the Blonde: Fairy Tales and Their Tellers* (1994).

Porno/perverse sex has long been set up in tantalising if simplistic opposition to boring ole vanilla sex, so perhaps reading *Beige* simply offers the pleasure of sampling taboo material. More slap than tickle. Naughty but nice!

Perhaps *Beige* carries additional, hidden meanings. Bestsellers are held to dramatise mass unconscious wishes, after all. Since, in the unconscious, if not always in real life, we can be both 'masculine' and 'feminine', reading *Beige* we can imagine the sadist to be female as well as male, if we want to. Does *Beige* allow its female readers to reclaim the aggression they're not supposed to possess or enjoy in real life?

Perhaps, also, *Beige* lets readers rehearse their lived experiences of humiliation in childhood at the hands of parents (the so-called compulsion to repeat) and so lets them hope to transcend them.[19] Or does reading *Beige* simply, consolingly, confirm those scenarios as inevitable? It's not your fault. Nothing can change. Just keep dreaming.

Mothers, according to psychoanalysts such as Donald Winnicott, are supposed to gaze

19. See Alice Miller, *The Drama of the Gifted Child* (1979).

adoringly at their babies' faces. The baby finds himself or herself mirrored in the mother's gaze. If you haven't experienced enough of that loving attention, might you find it in the intense, intimate S&M scenario? The masochist adores her importance to the sadist, revels in her abjection, her permitted passivity. She is cherished and taken care of by the ever-inventive, ever-attentive sadist. Baby, baby, he whispers.[20]

Perhaps masochistic fantasies dramatise present wishes. Perhaps modern women, exhausted by having to be continually, actively responsible as wage-earners, captains of industry, mothers and carers, let alone wives, obliged to be so in control, so strong, so giving, sometimes yearn to lie back, passive and yielding, and be dandled by an ideal partner/mummy. *Beige* lets readers indulge that wish.

Beige has something for everyone!

Except jokes. (The sexiest short story I've ever read is 'The Obelisk', by E. M. Forster – not writing as Miss Lavish – because it is so funny. Its comedy involves confusion, mystery,

20. Cries of 'Bollocks! Bollocks!' from the back. I ignore them..

lying and bisexuality. Its erotic charge invokes Shakespearian playfulness and joy.)

Perhaps the S&M scenario of *Beige* simply (unconsciously) dramatises gender conflict within the human psyche and simultaneously muffles it. The times they are a'changin, but we can't all cope. Let's escape into a novel.

T he fact that becoming a Real Woman, that's to say a feminine woman, paradoxically involved artifice (suitable costumes, make-up and behaviour) meant that men could join in and play dressing up too. Some transvestites, donning pearls and cocktail frocks, seemed to be copying their mothers, perhaps identified with them. Others, more camp, opted for ball-gowns and bouffants, acting out feminine stereotypes with a more overtly ambivalent panto mix of affection and hostility.

Femininity has nowadays become literalised, re-written in female flesh. Reminding women that they are so much less than perfect, the market offers solutions. Femininity now involves radical bodily alteration, cosmetic surgical

interventions such as facelifts, breast enhance-
ments, lip enlargements, buttocks-sculpting,
labia shaping, etc., marketed to women as nor-
mal practices following on from women's natural, healthy desire for self-improvement and
empowerment.[21] It seems to follow, therefore,
that given modern developments in surgical
technology and hormonal treatments you can
become a Real Woman even if you've started
off as a man.

(The operation can also, of course, work the
other way round.)

Is there some confusion here? Has sex become identified with gender all over again?
Some feminists arouse outrage and fury by
suggesting that perhaps some trans people
have been trapped less in the wrong body than
in restrictive notions of gender. For example,
in *Slipshod Sibyls* (1995), discussing women's
poetry but ranging across other literary forms,
Germaine Greer asserts 'Both men and women
are tormented by the disjunction between their
gender and their sex, but it is not women who

21. Far-seeing Fay Weldon satirised this development in her
novel *The Life and Loves of a She-Devil* (1984).

48

have constructed the masculinity that so many men find a bad fit.'

If a boy or man wants to be more 'feminine' does he have to undergo an operation? Or could he live out his fantasies and wishes differently? Experiment with different outfits and hairdos and cheerfully, coolly, strut his ambiguous stuff? Invent a fictional female character and write a novel told from her first person point of view?

Greer seems to be saying that first we need to accept our sexed bodies and then try to live the fullest, richest lives possible, thereby overcoming cultural expectations of conventional masculine/feminine roles: 'Only by the full disclosure of sex potentiality can the miserable fraud that is gender be seen for what it is.'[22]

In the past, women's discomfort with being put in their place could lead to political engagement; collective feminist struggles for social justice. Now, in an age of renewed, severe gender prescription and consequent anxiety and unhappiness, the solution is presented as individual choice. If you feel like a misfit, you don't

22. Germaine Greer, *Slipshod Sybils* (1995), p. 101.

have to try to change the world. You can just change yourself. However, some trans people, newly made into beautiful women, do then find they have to become feminists. Unequal pay, sexual exploitation and violence, the sexual double standard, have not been magicked away.

The new identity politics renews old questions around authority, naming, labelling, hierarchies of belonging. Is biological sex the same as constructed sex or is it truer and better or doesn't that difference matter? Defenders and opponents fight it out.[23] These heated disagreements and skirmishes, sometimes becoming over-simplified, remind me of the Christian patriarchs opposing the heretics. You're either with us or against us! If you criticise us we'll punish you! Silence!

What effect do these debates about sexual and gender identity have on our imaginations? Do they inspire us or discompose us or do both?

Will the new stress on literalness make

23. For example, see the letters pages of the *London Review of Books*, 2016, *passim*.

metaphors vanish, stop us trusting our imaginations? Will True Life memoirs wipe fiction off the map?

Writing novels (the traditional sort, anyway) involves going beyond the personal ego and imagining being someone else; often someone of the opposite sex. Imagination here overlaps with empathy. If certain groups of people who reject old-style binary identities feel that they have been silenced, will they welcome novelists claiming their empathetic right to write about them?

Will those of us who've enjoyed investigating and playing with gender in the past find new, different stories to tell? I hope so.

Rack Press Editions is an imprint of Rack
Press Poetry, which has published nearly forty
contemporary poets in quality limited editions.

In 2014 Rack press won the Michael Marks Award
for poetry pamphlet Publisher of the Year.

'Rack Press ever impresses' – *Poetry Review*
'The consistently reliable Rack Press'
– *Times Literary Supplement*

From Rack Press Editions:

Nicholas Murray
Bloomsbury and the Poets

Jeremy Noel-Tod
*The Whitsun Wedding Video:
A journey through British poetry*

THE RACK PRESS POETS

Nicky Arscott
John Barnie
A. C. Bevan
Byron Beynon
Siobhán Campbell
Peter Dale
Damian Walford Davies
Martina Evans
Katy Evans-Bush
Hazel Frew
John Greening
Steve Griffiths
Susan Grindley
Eve Grubin
David Harsent
Rosalind Hudis
David Kennedy
Anna Lewis
Andrew McCulloch
Philip Morre

Nicholas Murray
Katrina Naomi
William Palmer
Ian Parks
Fiona Pitt-Kethley
Ian Pople
Richard Price
Christopher Reid
Michèle Roberts
Fiona Sampson
Denise Saul
Deirdre Shanahan
Róisín Tierney
Angela Topping
Dai Vaughan
John Powell Ward
David Wheatley
Dan Wyke
Samantha
Wynne-Rhydderch